Agape Voice

PILLOW TALKS

Agape Voice Publishing
277 West 4th Street
Charlotte, NC 28202

Manufactured in the United States of America

This book is dedicated to Love.

You Must Be Brave

Who said you can't write a book? Who said your story is not compelling enough? Who said it was too expensive? Who said keep your day job? Who said "no" to you? Well, we want you to take all those individuals that spoke life out of your book and remove yourself from them; maybe just while you write. We don't want you to argue or try to convince anyone that you have a book in you anymore because that is doing nothing but holding up your process. We want you to close the door to language that doesn't support your writing journey because now is the time, but you must be brave. Yes, you must be brave to write a book. You can't be distracted by judgement or insecurity. You can't care what people think and you can't play "the blame game" if anything comes short. You must own your book, no matter who begins or ends with you on this journey.

Begin with the truth in your heart and ask yourself what you want to write about. The beginning is deciding. Most of us have thousands of stories in us but we are going to just start with one for this guide. And that one story may have 5 books in it. Yet, ***Agape Voice*** encourages simplicity and clarity, so let's start with the book you are most passionate about. This book needs to be well understood by you and easy for you to tell orally.

This book needs to have a good plot or clear steps to follow. You see if you don't know what you are talking about no one else will know what you are talking about. So, keep it simple and be open to learn.

Let's talk about genre for a minute. We know that fiction is not "real", and non-fiction is real but there are many genres inside these categories. So, when you think about the two, I want you to reflect on the story you are writing. Is it full of lies? Is it a guide? Is it a suspense piece? Is it inspiring? Here is a list of genres. Using the number "1" as the genre that interests you the most and 10 for the genre that interests you the least, put a number beside each. If you don't see your genre on the list, add it.

Realistic Fiction	_____	Urban Fiction	_____
Historical Fiction	_____	Informational	_____
Science Fiction	_____	Fantasy	_____
Poetry	_____	Mystery	_____
Biography	_____	Autobiography	_____

Only take 1 minute for this because writing is about setting timelines and sticking to it.

Self-Publishing vs. Being Published by a firm
That is the question.

Agape Voice takes book submissions throughout the year. We read dozens of pieces weekly and in this competitive process, we choose the pieces that we believe will make the most money and inspire the audience. We fund and sponsor these projects to build our brand. All submissions are reviewed using the books synopsis which we will discuss in later chapters. We do not guarantee a writer is eligible for this process and this is contracted.

Now, self-Publishing is very different. There are many companies that offer self-publishing services, and this is for a fee. Services such as editing, proofreading, converting writings to a Word Doc or PDF, formatting can be purchased in a package or *a-la-carte*. A deposit is required to begin self-publishing options.

Transcriber

A transcriber is someone that takes your account word for word and puts it into print. Nothing is changed from what you say. These services are based on pages and can start at $200.

Ghostwriter

A ghostwriter is someone that writes your book for you. This is a very intricate process that requires a consultation. These services start at $3500.00 and are subject to approval.

Writers Toolbox
Step 1

"You can make anything by writing." – C.S. Lewis

Writing can be a hobby. Writing can be a craft. Writing can be a profession. Writing can be a career. Writing can be a lifestyle. It's all up to you. Deciding your literary path takes great thought and reflection and ***Agape Voice*** is here to help you make a few decisions on this awesome journey.

The first step is to pack your toolbox. Yes, a toolbox which you may be carrying for 90 days, 6 months, 2 years or even a decade because you are the carpenter of this masterpiece. Some describe writing as building a house, with each word holding up a splendid piece of the home. For me it was building an ark and I was Noahesa; dazed and confused. I couldn't keep up with all the animals on the boat and everyone laughed and mocked me when I told them to come aboard. You see I wrote my first book to escape pain without considering, process or support (remember those words). I published a memoire of sorts filled with jumbled thoughts and incomplete ideas and my boat sunk shortly after leaving shore.

Well, we will help you to avoid these and other pitfalls. We are here for you before you even break ground and there is some equipment you need to collect before starting your project.

For your first book I suggest you create a piece of furniture versus a house. What I mean by this is keep your book under 100 pages. Learn the art of writing. Seek clarity and order in your piece. Make a statement and a point that will encapsulate your audience and not exhaust them out of reading. We don't want any books that we publish to collect dust on a shelf.

This guide is a great example of a first-time book and included in our toolbox were notepads, pens, highlighters, white out, a laptop, a logo, chocolate and peppermint candy sticks. Now this is a personalized Dearest and Katris toolbox. Tell me some things that you think you need in your toolbox. Use your five senses. What inspires or facilitates you to write. Please list at least 5 items. Take only 3 minutes

- ______________________________________
- ______________________________________
- ______________________________________
- ______________________________________
- ______________________________________
- ______________________________________

Now that you have a toolbox, it's time to continue to build on that idea. Make sure your story is strong. Always incorporate the "who, what, why, where, when" questions to build interest.

A few extra tips:

- *Write a certain amount of words daily. This builds writing muscle. I started my writing journey with 500 hundred words, now my average is 3000 daily.*
- *Choose a location that is inviting and comfortable to write in each day.*
- *Pack your toolbox with pictures, candy, candles and other items that stimulate the soul.*

Prewriting/Sorting through the Mess/Planning and Plotting Step 2

"When can you start calling yourself a writer? NOW." – Anonymous

There are many planning strategies used to write a book. I am going to take one of my favorite and allow you to start your book with it. I call this method, "The See Forward Outline". The first thing a writer should do is create an outline. Do this before you look at any notebook, tissue paper, text or post that you have written. Make a title for each chapter that you are trying to write before you write it but make the chapters backwards. Meaning, what happened last is first.

Here is an example for the "Three Little Pigs".

1. Never Seen Again
2. Wolf Gets His Butt Burned
3. Sliding Down the Chimney
4. Brick House
5. House of Sticks
6. House of Straw
7. Pigs Set Out for Independence

Now you practice. Think of a story you would like to write or one that is familiar to you. Give it an end, a middle and a beginning using titles. If you have trouble outlining backwards, start with title 7 and make your way up.

1. ____
   ____
2. ____
   ____
3. ____
   ____
4. ____
   ____
5. ____
   ____
6. ____
   ____
7. ____
   ____

Take 5 Minutes to Finish.

This is just a draft outline, a starting point. You may use another method to get started but this outline secures that you finish the race. As you go through all the writing drafts that you may have accumulated, you have a pathway to put the information in your book. Knowing where your book ends is essential in completing the project. This enables you to see forward in order to get to your destination.

Combing Through the Mess

Many of you have sheets of paper, notebooks, tissue, files that consist of material that you want to put in your book. It may be very organized or in shambles. In any case you can use a colored highlighter/pencil to put those pages in order based on your chapter title. An example is put use a yellow highlight for everything that goes in chapter 1. Maybe a blue highlight for 2 and so on and so forth. Colored pencils, sticky notes, highlighters are all excellent items for your toolbox.

A few extra tips:

- *Create a plot outline based on what will happen next.*
- *Always reference back to your outline.*
- *Create a character grind which will remind you of persons in the text.*

Write, Revise, Release

Step 3

"The first draft is just telling yourself the story." – Terry Pratchett

Now it is time to write. Set a daily goal and stick to it. Please prepare yourself to write in a Word or Google document. Most firms will not take anything handwritten. ***Agape Voice*** does offer services to transfer your writings to these documents. The starting rate for these services is $200. Try to write in the same location each day, having your toolbox as support. Be reflective with your words and remember the first go around is just a draft. Don't beat yourself up. Tune into what is relevant about what you are writing. For example, if you are writing about home cooking, have your recipes ready. Pictures and visuals are always excellent to use to bring color and life to your story. As you write, be connected to your five senses (see, smell, touch, taste, hear).

Let's tune into our senses to incorporate into our writing. Using simile, which is, "a figure of speech involving the comparison of one thing with another thing of a different kind, used to make a description more emphatic or vivid." (Oxford), let's describe colors. It is the use of "like" or "as." An example is, "red as the blood that poured from his veins."

Now it's your turn. Using simile, describe these words.

Blue____

Red____

Green_______________________________________

Black_______________________________________

Yellow______________________________________

Orange______________________________________

Brown_______________________________________

Take 4 Minutes

Metaphor is a figure of speech that is often used in writing. "It is a word or phrase that is applied to an object or action to which it is not literally applicable." (Oxford). Ex. "*It's raining cats and dogs.*" Now, come up with a metaphor of your own now.

Take 2 Minutes

The stories we tell should be colorful bringing sound off the pages. The aroma should move the reader while the feeling they get should always be moving. Don't just write words. Be overly descriptive, leaving no stone unturned. Make sure the reader can see without eyes to see.

Now of course this may not apply to informational pieces but stirring interest is very important in all text.

Revise

How often should a writer revise? I say no more than 3 times. The first revision is completely necessary. The second is to catch what you may have missed. The third is you are entering the territory of obsession and if you don't stop, you will never finish your book.

Release

Release your piece to one and said one, trustworthy person that is a reader. Let them give you feedback before you go to editing.

A few extra tips:

- *Going back to earlier chapters; "Be Brave".*
- *Don't look for perfection but be authentic.*
- *Utilize your toolbox. Go back to the chapter and add more onto your list.*
- *Let your senses be your guide.*

Synopsis

Step 4

"And by the way, everything in life is writable about if you have the outgoing guts to do it, and the imagination to improvise. The worst enemy to creativity is self-doubt." – Sylvia Plath

Your book is done. You have outlined, drafted, revised and released the piece. Now it's time to summarize it in a synopsis so you will be marketable for print. A synopsis is, "a brief summary or general survey of your book" (Oxford).

Most publishing firms, including ***Agape Voice***, will need for you to have your book summarized to even consider publishing. As mentioned in prior chapters, clarity and order is essential to putting out a successful product. It is usually only 3 to 4 pages, single spaced and is written in the third person. It starts by introducing the main characters, conflict, plot and resolution. It only includes necessary information and it is not subjective, meaning you should never compliment your work. This is very important because many authors write attempting to impress the reader. A synopsis is a piece where the book must stand on its' own. Please make sure you check your formatting requirements for the firm that you will be submitting this to. This is essential to getting your work passed along but is not necessary for self-published authors who are paying out of pocket for all of their services.

Make sure when you have your synopsis completed you have someone with a good eye read it over. You can also opt to get a synopsis edited. This is a service that ***Agape Voice*** provides.

A few extra tips:

- *Avoid plagiarism at all cost. We have a database that checks words that have already have a copyright. Always avoid, pictures, phrases, words that you don't give the originator credit for or you haven't purchased.*
- *Invest in editing which is discussed below. It is the difference between a book that's read by 20 people and a best seller.*
- *Self-published authors are sole proprietors over their work and **Agape Voice** is not liable for what goes to print.*

Editing/Cover Charge
At the House and Professionally
Step 5

"You can always edit a bad page. You can't edit a blank page." – Jodi Picoult

You are your first editor. You need to edit at home before you pass your piece to a professional editor. Yet, professional editing is always recommended. In lengthy pieces you will always miss something. ***Agape Voice***, has editors on site and our charges start at $200.

Cover Charge

Although this may be the time your cover is created, we believe that the imagery or art on the cover should be brainstormed throughout the process of writing the book. You have different options for your cover. You can use an illustrator. We have several on staff to make your cover original. You can also use a photo or purchase a photo. Copyright rules apply. Covers start at $350.

A few extra tips:

- *Editing cleans up your work. Make sure you use a professional.*

- *Your cover is the first thing the reader sees. Make sure it pops off the page and interests the reader in purchasing your book.*

Communicating Your Message

Step 6

"Read a thousand books. And your words will flow like a river." – Lisa See

I was very shocked once my strategist informed me that I had more work to do after I wrote a 10-chapter book! "What" I stated, "there is more work to do".

Many authors are under the false impression that a book sells itself or a book will be read. Well, no.

In order to have a successful journey as an author there are three main ingredients to add to your book. Just look at your book as the flour or the foundation of a yummy cake. Just imagine...there would be no cake without the flour. But the sugar frosting and other ingredients bring flavor. Your book must have flavor! And in order to sell your book you must have a target/aim, confidence and GPS. Hit Your Target "Aim High"

You must understand that we all have an audience. Your book should carry a very specific message. This message should be delivered to a particular audience.
For example: Cookbooks are created for those who love to cook or desire to learn how to cook. I would not be

interested in a cookbook. I have no real desire at this moment to learn any recipes. However, there is a massive of people who enjoy cooking. These individuals would be considered your audience.

Once you know your audience, you must target ONLY those individuals. Other people will purchase your book to show support or maybe just because they like the book cover but stay focused on your audience. Target your audience directly.

When you have a target mindset, you actually step into a zone where your communication is So relatable to them that you eventually gain a "distant" relationship with your audience. And once you gain a relationship with your audience...it is good business for you! Aim as high as you can!

When you start targeting your audience, I need you to aim high! Become the expert for the people who need you. Your book is important to those who need to hear what you are saying, so do not play low. Aim high.

For example: If you wrote a book on 4 secrets to help mother's lose weight, you must present your book with value and excellence to those who need to hear what you are sharing. Have a high expectation that your audience need to hear what you have to say.

Aim High:

Create a standard and place value on your words.

Who is your audience?

____

What do your audience look like?

____

____

Where would you find your audience?

____

____

Session 2: Confidence in your voice!

Session 3: Stay in your lane!

Session 4: Show up!

Publishing Options

Step 7

Published Authors
Steps to being Published

Submit a Synopsis which Includes:

- Title
- Written in the Third Person
- Summary of main events of plot
- Resolution
- Only Necessary Information
- Character Development
- Not Complementary

Package for Independent Authors
7 Steps to Self-Publishing

Step 1 - Submit Manuscript which Includes:

- Title
- The Acknowledgements
- The Forward
- Preface
- Introduction
- Prologue
- Completed document, book or work

Step 2 – Editing which includes, copy editing, proofreading, formatting and review.

Substantive editing can be performed at an additional charge.

- Copy editing, where we correct problems of grammar, style, repetition, word usage, and jargon.
- Proofreading is the lightest form of editing, where minor errors are corrected.

- Formatting will amend document text to ensure that it complies with the required format.
- Review is where the editor may provide a one to two-page glance of the book.
- **Substantive (developmental) editing. The most intensive form of editing. This is where the document is evaluated "as a whole" and problems of structure, organization, coherence, and local consistency are corrected. Sentences may be removed or added. Paragraphs may be rewritten, condensed, or expanded. Blocks of text may be moved from one section to another.*

Step 3 - Book Cover Design

- Consult with design team about ideas. Submit photos and other materials to design your cover.
- Design
- Review
- Approve

Step 4 – Send to Print

- Upload Book for Print and e-book
- Give a projective time to author

Step 5 – Basic Rights Licensing

Step 6 – Review Book

- Similar to proofreading

Step 7 – Promote/Market Book

- Social Media Pages and Groups
- 1 Press Release
- 1 Blog Review
- 1 Ad in local printed publication
- 1 Radio Interview

Packages Start at $1700.00

www.agapevoice1@gmail.com

You Must Be Brave

"Bravery is the audacity to be unhindered by failures, and to walk with freedom, strength, and hope in the face of things unknown."

~Morgan Warner Michaels

Made in the USA
Columbia, SC
12 March 2020

89077828R00015